LYMINGTON-YARMOUTH
The New Generation

John Hendy

GW00647407

WIGHTLINK

Published by
Ferry Publications,
PO Box 33,
Ramsey,
Isle of Man
IM99 4LP
Tel: 01624 898446
Fax: 01624 898449
E-mail: ferrypubs@manx.net
Website: www.ferrypubs.co.uk

FOREWORD

The shortest route to the Isle of Wight has always been the most demanding in terms of providing purpose-built ships in order to meet the stringent requirements and limitations of the Lymington River.

Prior to the opening of Lymington Pier in 1884, the service was of necessity tidal in nature but the deep-water berths gave the route a new impetus and tonnage grew larger as a result of the improved arrangements. Even then, new paddle steamers caused initial concerns as their larger deckhouses caught the wind and in certain conditions they were difficult to navigate through the sweeping meanders of the lower Lymington River.

During the twentieth century, the dramatic growth of cars being carried on the route demanded a total reassessment of how that traffic should be carried. The car ferry *Lymington* of 1938 proved to be the answer and carrying 20 cars and powered by the revolutionary Voith-Schneider propulsion units, the ship could be manoeuvred in any direction thereby earning her the nickname of 'The Crab.' The *Lymington* soon showed any doubters that their fears were unfounded.

In 1973, the 'C' class ferries were introduced and proved to be the largest ferries yet. They have been extremely successful ships and regular travellers on the route owe them a great debt of gratitude for their reliability, comfort and longevity. However, with the imposition of even greater demands being made on ship operators concerning damage stability, combined with the long service of the 'C' class, new ships eventually became a necessity.

The design of the new 'Wight' class was formulated after many hours of consultation involving all interest groups and after extensive tank tests to determine the ideal hull shape which would keep wash to a minimum in the Lymington River.

Wightlink is 100% committed to the Lymington – Yarmouth route. The new ships are larger than the 'C' class but their increased capacity is essential to help secure the long-term viability of this historic route.

Without doubt, the new 'Wight' class will introduce higher and more comfortable standards of travel than ever before and with improved fuel efficiency and lower emissions, their green footprint will be the envy of other operators in the region. The 'Wight' class represent a huge commitment from Wightlink Isle of Wight Ferries.

This publication sets out to place the new ships in the context of the Lymington – Yarmouth route and shows how it has grown and evolved to reach its present day state. It covers a fascinating period of maritime history and I am confident that the 'Wight' class will play their full part in the route's continuing success.

Andrew Willson
Chief Executive Officer – Wightlink Isle of Wight Ferries

INTRODUCTION

The Wight Light waiting off Yarmouth Pier during her trials in September 2008. (John Hendy)

The three and a half miles across the Western Solent between Lymington and Yarmouth have always required specially designed ships of shallow draught. The historic route is undoubtedly one of the most demanding in the country and its sturdy and diminutive vessels have all reflected this fact.

The faithful and reliable 'C' Class ferries have served the passage for over thirty years and have given an impressive period of service. However, times have moved on, the demands of the route's customers have changed and ongoing legislation regarding Safety of Life at Sea (SOLAS) has meant that if this popular service was to continue, then new tonnage would be required to operate it.

The ships were duly ordered from a Croatian yard in March 2007 and named *Wight Light, Wight Sky* and *Wight Sun* - the winning entries in a competition held by owners Wightlink.

This celebratory publication aims to tell the story of the crossing from the commencement of steam navigation in 1830 until the present day and describes the challenge and construction of the three new ships.

Thus a further chapter is about to be unveiled concerning the shortest and most picturesque route to the Isle of Wight.

John Hendy
Plovers, Ivychurch, Romney Marsh, Kent

September 2008

LYMINGTON – YARMOUTH

THE WESTERN LINK

Wightlink's Lymington to Yarmouth route is in many ways the back door to the Isle of Wight. Whereas the links from Portsmouth represent a great transition, sailing from a noisy and sprawling urban area to the wooded and open shores of the 'Garden Isle,' the Lymington route is altogether gentler as the wild and beautiful New Forest gives way to the forest of masts in the busy yacht haven. As one sails the three and a half miles across to Yarmouth, the spectacular backdrop of the whale-backed downs never fails to inspire and the little town itself exudes a salty Georgian respectability.

The quiet Hampshire market town of Lymington is not really the place where one would expect to find a busy ferry terminal but over a million passengers each year pass through on their way to or from the island.

The route has always provided problems with navigation. On setting off, the Lymington River's deep-water channel meanders through an extensive region of salt marsh that culminates in Cocked-Hat Corner where wind and tide have caused so many groundings through the years. Today's Wightlink vessels are both powerful and highly manoeuvrable and they certainly need to be in order to maintain their busy and demanding schedules.

Once out of the confines of the Lymington River, in which the constant comings and goings of yachtsmen of all abilities also present problems of a different nature, the passage to Yarmouth crosses the Western Solent. Here one catches sight of Hurst Castle at

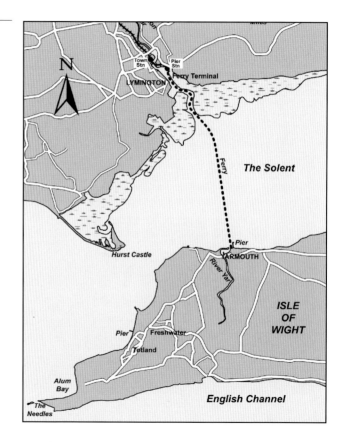

the end of its long shingle spit, while beyond, the distant Needles stand defiantly against the remorseless pounding of the grey English Channel. The prevailing south-westerly winds and the strong tidal currents which rush through the narrow entrance to the Solent can cause serious difficulties for small vessels crossing the ebb and flow of the shortest route to the island.

THE PORTS

As its name implies, Yarmouth lies at the estuary of the River Yar which was crossed by ferry until a road bridge was built in 1863. The origins of the town go back to 991 when it was called Eremue meaning 'muddy estuary' but it was the Normans who laid out the streets in their familiar grid pattern. The town became a parliamentary borough during the Middle Ages and until the Reform Act of 1832, the Yarmouth constituency was represented by two Members of Parliament.

Yarmouth was the first town on the Isle of Wight to gain a Royal Charter in 1135 and was twice raided and sacked by the French in 1377 and 1524. There were so many invasions during this period that landowners were in the habit of sending their wives and families across to the mainland for safety and there was concern that the island would become seriously depopulated. The security of the local residents was greatly improved in 1547 when Henry VIII built Yarmouth Castle as one of a chain of fortifications in the Solent area.

The wooden pier dates from 1876, the year after the garrison was withdrawn from the castle, and is a Grade II listed building. The Lymington ferry service used the pier from the time of its construction until the withdrawal of the last passenger steamer in

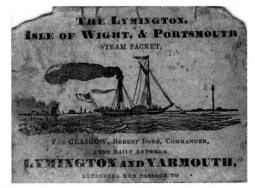

An early sailing bill for the Lymington, Isle of Wight and Portsmouth Steam Packet vessel Glasgow showing a drawing of the ship. (The St. Barbe Museum, Lymington)

An early steamer, believed to be the Red Lion, making her way up the Lymington River to the Town Station Slipway. (The St. Barbe Museum, Lymington)

1959 although ever since the days of the tow-boats, the car ferry traffic has always been handled at the entrance to the harbour on the western side of the castle. The population of Yarmouth is about 1,000 and although it boasted a railway station between 1889 and 1953, the line between Freshwater and Newport by-passed the quay, traffic was always light and its influence on the ferry route was therefore negligible.

Lymington can trace its origins back to the sixth century when it was called Limen Tun, a Celtic name meaning 'marshy river'. By the time of the Domesday Book (1086) it was known as Lentune and was later made a town and given the right to hold markets by the Lord of the Manor.

From the Middle Ages onwards, Lymington became important for the manufacture of salt which was made either by boiling sea water in copper pots or by allowing it to evaporate in trapped ponds or saltpans. A healthy coastwise trade developed and the town became a prosperous port; wine was imported from France and Salisbury cloth was exported. Just as with Yarmouth, the town was sacked twice by the French during the One Hundred Years War and again in 1545.

During the seventeenth century boat building increasingly gained in importance. This gradually developed into yacht building but the decline of the salt industry in the mid-nineteenth century caused great hardship and was responsible for a fall in population during

Seen shortly after the opening of Lymington Pier station in May 1884, the square sterned Solent (II) heads up the Lymington River with a tow boat astern. A train of four-wheeled carriages waits at the station. (The St. Barbe Museum, Lymington)

The Solent of 1863 (left) and the Mayflower of 1866 alongside the new railway at Lymington. Built three years apart, their design appears almost identical. The latter steamer is on the 1861 jetty with her stern facing the Lymington Town Wharf Slipway from where the tow boat service was operated. (John Hendy collection)

this period. Daniel Defoe had described Lymington as a town, 'chiefly noted for making fine salt, which is indeed excellent good' and in the early nineteenth century the local salt trade was second only in importance to that of Liverpool. The industry at Lymington declined quickly as rock salt was discovered in Cheshire and local manufacturers using solar evaporation failed to compete against the industrial might of the north west of England.

Today Lymington is perhaps best known for its connection with yachts and yachting. The Lymington River Sailing Club was founded in 1914 and finally gained its Royal Warrant in 1938. The population of this bustling market town is about 35,000.

Until the car ferry service commenced at Lymington Pier in 1938, the earlier system of conveying vehicles by tow boat was worked from a slipway up river at what eventually became known as Lymington Town Station Wharf.

EARLY DAYS

Although for many years the Lymington to Yarmouth route had been maintained by local rowing boats and sailing wherries, it was the locally owned and wooden-hulled *Glasgow* (51 tons), under the command of Captain Robert Dore, which opened the crossing to steam navigation on 5th April 1830. The vessel had been built two years earlier at John Wood's yard at Port Glasgow which had also produced the pioneering steam ship *Comet* in 1812.

During March 1830, the 16 horse power paddle steamer was purchased by a consortium led by three Lymington businessmen. Charles and Samuel St. Barbe were bankers and owners of a local salt factory and Edward Hicks was also a banker. Their new ship

measured just 53 feet 6 inches long but made the short crossing in a very respectable 30 minutes 'with only half her power on'. The local newspaper reported that she had a bowsprit, a 'billet' head, one striking mast, a square stern and quarter badges. As the road communications in the Solent region were so poor, for three days each week these early services were extended to serve Cowes, Ryde and Portsmouth and to Southampton via Yarmouth and Cowes on the other three while Sundays were spent on service to Yarmouth only. In May 1831, the *Glasgow* was lengthened by 6 feet.

Compared with today's standards, facilities were primitive. At low tide, the lack of water at Lymington Town Quay brought delays while

The Mayflower at lay-up in the Lymington River . The pontoon in the right foregound was used by the halfpenny ferry which took passengers across the river to the Town Quay. (Tom Lee collection)

Top left: The Mayflower (left) and the Lymington. Of particular interest is the absence of the latter's after First Class deck saloon which appears to have been added at a later date - presumably to complement the facilities of the 1902 Solent. (R.B. Adams collection)

Top middle: The Lymington of 1893 was the London & South Western Railway's first steamer for the route. Apart from a canvas 'dodger' the Captain was provided with no protection and overall the ship offered the majority her Third Class passengers (forward) little in the way of shelter. (Tom Lee collection)

Top right: The Lymington on tow boat duty at her berth on the 1861 jetty adjacent to the Station Wharf Slipway. (Tom Lee Collection)

Left: Taken from the 1861 pier, a formal photograph believed to be of Lord Montague of Beaulieu and the first carriage of a motor car from Lymington to Yarmouth. The car is already loaded on the tow boat at the Town Station Slipway. (Bert Moody collection)

Yarmouth was extremely exposed and it was not until 1847 that the breakwater was completed thereby giving the harbour some much-needed shelter. Lymington's tidal restraints meant that passengers were ferried out in small boats to the waiting steamers but even at high tide, congestion at the Town Quay could mean them having to clamber over other vessels before reaching the Yarmouth ship.

For many years cargo was transferred to the Isle of Wight in specially constructed tow boats (also called horseboats), which looked like half-barges with a gate across the flat end. The hinged gates would be lowered to form a ramp and the addition of planks made for an acceptable connection with the shore. The tow boats handled livestock, goods and later cars over a slipway and were usually pulled by the service steamer or a specially chartered tug. The first of the tow boats was introduced in May 1836 and proved to be a great innovation, especially as the travelling public were no longer required to share the decks of their ships with frightened farm animals on their way to market. However, during periods of bad weather when the tow boats were unable to be pulled, passengers frequently found themselves sharing the accommodation with the odd pig or cow. The 'Lymington Chronicle' had complained of sheep being carried and, 'rendering the deck a nuisance to every person on board.' Fortunately this practice has long since ceased but the tow boats continued in use on a daily basis until the advent of the route's first car ferry in 1938.

An early advertisement for the *Glasgow's* services also mentions 'two commodious tow boats for the conveyance of horses, carriages and cattle.' One was stationed at Lymington and the other at Yarmouth 'for the greater convenience of the public' and to 'prevent delay.'

Sailings from Lymington were four times a day every Tuesday, Thursday and Saturday at 09.00, 11.00, 15.00 and 18.00 while return crossings were advertised at 10.00, 12.00, 16.00 and 18.30. It was noted that, 'The above arrangements will be observed with the utmost punctuality.' The ship offered two classes – the wealthy travelled in the partial comfort and protection of the Quarter-deck and paid 1s (5p) for the privilege. The poorer classes were charged 9d (4p) for travelling in the Forecastle which would certainly have been rather wet at times and also shared with any travelling livestock. Children under 10 were charged half price.

The artist's impression of the ship heading towards Lymington (see page 5) is also worthy of closer study. As with many of the earlier steamers, a sail was always carried in case of mechanical failure although even the paddle steamer *Freshwater* of 1927 carried a small sail for ease of manoeuvring in the confines at Lymington.

The larger *Solent* (61 tons) came on station during the summer of 1841 having been specifically built for the route at Northam, Southampton, by Summers, Groves and Day. The Solent Sea Steam Packet Company was formed to operate the service. Launched on 18th May 1841, the *Solent's* entry into service saw the smaller and older *Glasgow* relegated to the thrice-daily - two on Sundays - ferry crossing while the new ship maintained the longer Solent passages. The *Solent* certainly created a good impression and a newspaper cutting dated 1842 referred to her as, 'the admired, new and fast iron packet steamer' which was then operating three times weekly from Lymington to Yarmouth, Cowes, Ryde and Portsmouth. Single masted, sloop rigged and 84 feet long, her Master was Captain J.M. Cribb.

As they carried the mail to the Isle of Wight, both vessels were referred to as Royal Mail Steam Packets and in April 1842 the *Glasgow* broke from routine when she carried hundreds of sightseers on an excursion to Totland Bay where a 71 ft. fin whale had been washed up on the beach. The poor creature eventually became one of the original tourist attractions at Blackgang Chine.

A fascinating original document in the St Barbe Museum at Lymington dated 1845, is an invoice made out to The Solent Sea Steam Packet Company by Summers Day and Baldock, Engineers and Iron Ship Builders. This concerned the *Solent's* annual refit which cost £171 4s 2d (£171.21) and the building of a new horseboat (tow boat) for £6 0s 2d (£6.01).

By the end of that decade, in September 1849 the *Glasgow* had been withdrawn from service and offered for sale and was adapted as a tug. There was no buyer and the steamer was eventually broken up in October 1852.

In anticipation of the increased traffic which the new railway would bring, the two-year old *Red Lion* - 54 gross tons and built by Thorburn and Alman of North Shields - was purchased from the Admiralty and introduced during June 1858. She was to give good service until her own sale in 1880 and was a single-masted, sloop-rigged vessel with a round stern and a 29 horse power engine. The vessel served for six more years as a tug at South Shields.

THE RAILWAY ARRIVES

In the following month, July 1858, the privately promoted Lymington Railway was opened, running down from a junction west of Brockenhurst (on the London & South Western Railway's main line from London to Bournemouth), to Lymington – a distance of some five miles. The railway had received its Royal Assent on 7th July 1856 and at first the London & South Western Railway showed little interest in the concern. The first train ran at 07.15 on 12th July and was given a rousing send off by the town band while local church bells rang out in celebration.

Traffic continued to grow and after twenty years of service, the *Solent* was withdrawn in 1861 and was replaced in November 1863 by a larger steamer of the same name. The new 85 feet long *Solent* (61 gross tons) was actually built locally by G. & I. Inman at Lymington but was towed to Southampton for her engines to be fitted. Captain Cribb was again in command when, with the Directors on board, he took the new ship on her maiden voyage to Stokes Bay and back during November. The year 1861 had seen the railway company open a small jetty down river from Lymington Town station at which the Yarmouth steamers now berthed. The pier was ideally situated for tow boat duties and was first used by the *Red Lion* in July that year. More importantly, its construction eased the problem of having to row passengers out to the waiting ferry at low water but even then problems could still occur during periods when the pier was occupied by other vessels.

During July 1866, there followed the 98 feet long iron-hulled *Mayflower* (69 tons), from Marshall Bros., Wellington Quay at Wallsend-on-Tyne. The ship's construction was supervised by Charles Hayball, chief engineer of the Solent Sea Steam Packet Company, she was powered by two oscillating engines totalling 40 horse power while her 'luxurious accommodation' was lit by stained glass skylights.

A sailing bill for May 1866 (Sundays excepted) shows four daily departures from Lymington at 08.30, 11.40, 15.00 and 18.35 while the return sailings from Yarmouth were timed at 09.15, 12.30, 16.35 and 19.15. Fares had increased to 1s 6d (7.5p) for the Quarter-deck and 1s (5p) for the Forecastle.

With the growth of the railway network and the ongoing improvements to land communications in the area, the sailings eastwards through the Solent were reduced to just one a week and the *Mayflower* commenced a summer daily service from Lymington – Yarmouth – Cowes – Ryde and Portsmouth in 1874. On one foggy night during her first season, the new *Mayflower* was unable to locate the entrance to the Lymington River and ran aground on a mud bank where she remained until the following morning.

The Solent about to berth at Yarmouth Pier during the 1920s with a varnished wheelhouse and brown-painted ventilators. (www.simplonpc.co.uk)

The London & South Western Railway (LSWR) took control of the Lymington Railway on 23rd March 1878 and in the following year the *Red Lion* was withdrawn from service and sold to South Shields owners in August 1880.

An important milestone in the route's history occurred on 1st May 1884 when the LSWR opened the extended branch line by half a mile across the river and onwards to Lymington Pier thereby allowing crossings to Yarmouth to be undertaken at all states of the tide. The *Mayflower* had the honour of operating the first sailing from the new pier from which four daily direct trains from Waterloo connected with the steamers with the tow boat service also leaving Lymington at 11.00 every morning.

Although it had received authorisation to run the steamer service in 1850, the railway company did not absorb it until July 1884 when the Solent Steamship Co's *Solent* and *Mayflower* along with four tow boats were acquired for the nominal sum of £2,750. The *Solent* was sold for £225 and broken up in Holland in June 1901 while the *Mayflower* was sold in June 1905 for only £50.

By the time that the railway had pushed on to Lymington Pier, some of the Yarmouth services had been extended to Totland while the odd one even went as far as Alum Bay Pier. Cruises too had become increasingly popular, Lymington Pier being ideally suited for excursionists to step straight from their trains and directly onto the waiting ships.

The LSWR's first ship for the route did not appear until 1893 and was named *Lymington*. She was built at Northam, Southampton by Day, Summers & Co. and was launched on 6th April. The £6,000 *Lymington* was the route's first ship with a steel hull and her accommodation received much praise with the main saloon being upholstered in Utrecht velvet and the ceilings painted in white and gold. Wooden panels of maple and oak completed the effect and at 120 feet long, the ship was able to accommodate 311 passengers. The *Lymington*'s maiden voyage was duly completed on 9th May.

On 7th December 1897, the Italian inventor Guglielmo Marconi experimented with wireless communication between the Royal Needles Hotel at Alum Bay and the elderly *Solent* which was lying off the Needles under the command of Captain H. Doe. The experiments were later extended to run from Alum Bay Pier to Bournemouth and Swanage and were shared by the *Mayflower*. South Westerly gales and dense fog certainly did not aid the ground-breaking work but the results showed that communication could be maintained whatever the motion of the ship.

A further ship, which was intended to be the third-named *Solent*, was ordered by the LSWR from the Mordey, Carney yard at Woolston, Southampton in December 1899. Progress on the £8,300 steamer's construction was evidently slow and the work appears to have been sub-contracted to a French shipbuilder. The vessel was finally delivered in January 1901 when it was discovered that she had failed to meet her contract requirements and her acceptance was refused.

Following legal proceedings, Mordey, Carney offered to build a replacement and the contract was finally sealed on 14th October 1901. The new ship was of 161 gross tons and of approximately the same dimensions as the earlier vessel but was not a direct repeat. The *Solent* (IV) was launched by Mrs. Lewis (wife of the Assisant Dockmaster) on 6th February 1902 before being handed over to her owners on 1st May.

Meanwhile, the rejected ship was purchased by the Metropolitan Asylums Board and named *Red Cross*. She was used as an ambulance steamer on the Thames but late in the First World War ferried workers in connection with the armaments depot at the Woolwich Arsenal.

After only four years in Mordey, Carney's hands, the Woolston yard was taken over by the well-known J. I. Thornycroft in June 1904.

The new *Solent* represented an advancement in that she introduced a Third Class deck saloon forward of the wheelhouse

A later view of the Solent passing down the Lymington River. She provided far more covered passenger accommodation than her predecessors and was fitted with an enclosed wheelhouse which also gave the Master a greater degree of protection from the elements. (Tom Lee collection)

A three-coach branch line train pulls into Lymington Pier station with passengers ready to board the Solent. (John Hendy collection)

which one would have expected to be welcomed by those connected with the route. However, the overall reaction to the new £9,000 steamer was initially quite the reverse due to the fact that in a strong blow, the deck saloon of the shallow draught vessel caught the full force of the wind and tended to drive her sideways, thereby making steering difficult. One Master is quoted as saying, 'Them glass houses pick up every puff o'wind; they're the very Dickens!' For this reason he preferred the old *Lymington* with her sharper keel and less superstructure.

In February 1906, the LSWR acquired the two-year old Dutch-built tug *Carrier* for tow boat duties thus relieving the service boat from this arduous task. It was stated that the vessel could carry up to 290 passengers but never appears to have been used in this capacity.

She remained in service until 1931 after which she was converted to a barge.

The year 1913 saw 700 cars landed at Yarmouth Quay by tow boat, a dramatic rise of 400 since 1907. It should be stated that during this time, the Western Solent route was far more popular with motorists and was more convenient than crossing from Portsmouth to Ryde. (The Portsmouth - Fishbourne route was not opened until March 1926.)

During the war, the service continued but although the Totland calls restarted in 1919, these were severely curtailed with the winter service closing in 1925 and the summer schedules finally being abandoned after 1927. The Alum Bay service closed in 1914, never to reopen.

SOUTHERN RAILWAY

The formation of the Southern Railway Company in 1923 saw continued growth and in 1927, the largest and final paddle steamer was added to the Lymington to Yarmouth route. This was the delightful *Freshwater* (264 gross tons) which was launched by Mrs. J.E.B. Seely, wife of the Lord Lieutenant of the county, at the East Cowes yard of J. Samuel White on 3rd May. The new steamer cost £22,500 to build, boasted far greater covered accommodation for her 500 passengers and entered service on 2nd June. First Class accommodation was found at her after end with the saloon on the Promenade Deck and the Ladies' Room on the Lower Deck. Third Class was forward with a saloon bar on the Lower Deck. The new ship was seen as the maximum size for safe navigation in the Lymington River and prior to her introduction, the Southern Railway spent £18,000 on dredging the channel and pier berths at Lymington.

Following the arrival of the *Freshwater*, the old *Lymington* was retired on 8th December 1927 but retained for pulling tow boats until following the acquisition of the tug *Jumsey* for these duties, she was disposed of in September 1929. Stripped of her engines and boiler the *Lymington* became a houseboat on the Hamble. She was then moved to Brundall on the Norfolk Broads and named *Glengarry* for a similar purpose before being sold again in October 1938 for use as a training ship for local Navy League Cadets at which time she became the *Lord Nelson*.

It was by this time becoming evident that the volume of motor car traffic was causing severe operational problems on the crossing. In 1930, vehicle numbers had risen to 1,650, this in spite of a drive on – drive off service having been introduced on the new Portsmouth - Fishbourne route in August 1927. Even today the route attracts many people simply because it is so different and provides a delightful alternative to those from the west of England or from the Midlands wishing to avoid the motorway network radiating from the M25.

There was much discussion and deliberation concerning the construction of a dedicated car ferry for Lymington but this was further complicated by the intervention of a new company. The Isle of Wight Ferry Co. announced that they were to start a new service from Keyhaven (west of Lymington) to Fort Victoria (the closest part of the island to the mainland) using two old Mersey vehicle ferries (or 'luggage boats' as they were known) which had become redundant following the opening of the Queensway Tunnel linking

The Solent alongside at Lymington Pier station and the Carrier heading down river with a tow boat en route to Yarmouth. (Bert Moody collection)

Liverpool with Birkenhead in 1934.

Initially the Southern Railway appeared interested in assisting the new company and much to the dismay of the Isle of Wight County Council, entered into negotiations with them. It was certainly an interesting idea but no funds were forthcoming to purchase the Mersey ferries and much time and effort was wasted before the Southern Railway finally announced that it was to build its own car ferry. Doubtless, the many supporters of the new car ferry service would have had their case strengthened by an incident that occurred on 16th July 1937. The *Solent* left Lymington as usual with the 12.15 service to Yarmouth towing a single barge loaded with two cars, a lorry and seven passengers. During the passage, the barge was in collision with the coaster *Obsidian* and although the people were thankfully picked up, the tow boat and its contents went down within two minutes and were lost.

CAR FERRIES

The revolutionary *Lymington* became the first British ferry to be powered by the Voith-Schneider method of propulsion that enabled her to move in any direction without rudders. Nicknamed 'The Crab,' she was built at the famous Scottish shipyard of Wm. Denny & Bros, Dumbarton and was able to carry some 430 passengers and 20 cars.

Much work was carried out on both sides of the Solent in preparation for the new ship. At Lymington, land was reclaimed, a concrete slipway and adjacent car park were built while the pier was widened and the station platform extended upstream to the new berth. Yarmouth also required a new slipway with adjacent timber pier whilst dredging was also essential before the new service could commence.

The double-ended *Lymington* entered service on 1st May 1938 being scheduled to operate seven round crossings each day and becoming the year-round workhorse on the passage. Serious technical problems were initially encountered with her new form of propulsion at which time the tow boat service was reactivated but her immediate success as a car carrier was obvious with just over 4,000 cars being carried in her first year compared with almost 2,500 in 1937.

A detailed view of the Carrier pulling towboats in the Lymington River. (Bert Moody collecion)

The Solent in mid-Solent with three tow boats astern and the destroyer HMS Wrestler heading for the English Channel. (Bert Moody collection)

The Southern Railway's Freshwater was the route's final paddle steamer and entered service in 1927. At almost 49 metres in length and with a capacity for 500 passengers, she was then claimed to be the largest steamer capable of navigating the Lymington River. (John Hendy collection)

The special slipways constructed on both sides of the Solent allowed cars to drive directly on and off the new ship while during the summer peak periods, the paddle steamer *Freshwater* would offer an additional service from Lymington Pier to Yarmouth Pier. With the new ferry in service, the *Solent* was downgraded and during the 1939 season only sailed on Saturdays, public holidays or when occasionally called in to relieve the *Freshwater* or *Lymington*.

During the Second World War, all sailings after dark were prohibited and the *Freshwater* sailed as far as Sheerness, arriving too late to assist in the Dunkirk Evacuation in early June 1940. At the close of that year she was requisitioned by the Royal Navy and spent most of her time as an examination ship at Weymouth and Portland.

Shortly after leaving Lymington on the evening of 10th August 1942, the *Lymington* was machine-gunned by a German Heinkel aircraft. The ship's own Lewis gun rattled into action and the adversary thankfully moved away. The elderly *Solent* narrowly escaped destruction at Southampton on 26th September 1940 when blazing timbers landed on her deck from a nearby warehouse and threatened to engulf her. Then, following the loss of the Portsmouth – Ryde steamer *Portsdown* when on passage in September 1941, she was sent to deputise while back at Lymington, in preparation for D Day the

The Freshwater shows a clean pair of heels as she leaves Yarmouth Pier in August 1959. (Norman Bird)

The Freshwater at the lay-by berth at the end of her career on the route when she was only being used on busy summer Saturdays. (Norman Bird)

slipway was doubled in width to allow two tank landing craft to load simultaneously. At this time the *Lymington* was moved up river to run a tidal service from the town slipway. Before hostilities had ceased, however, the Southern Railway had ordered a second car ferry for the Western Solent.

After a stormy passage south, the diesel-electric paddle vessel *Farringford* (named after Lord Tennyson's house near Freshwater) entered service for the nationalised British Transport Commission on 4th March 1948. She was also a product of Denny's Dumbarton yard and was the largest car ferry yet to serve the Western Solent route. At 178 feet long, she carried 320 passengers and 32 cars or as many as 800 passengers if serving as a passenger-only ship. Her extra beam

made her particularly unpopular with local yachtsmen both in the Lymington River and when alongside at Yarmouth Quay. In view of the serious problems experienced with the *Lymington's* Voith-Schneider propulsion system and its German construction so soon after the war, it was decided to fit her with independent paddle wheels driven by diesel-electric engines. After a few early problems during her first year in service when the *Freshwater* was reactivated to deputise, the arrangement worked well although she always lacked the manoeuvrability of the *Lymington*.

The old *Solent* of 1902 made her last regular sailings in 1947 and

The Lymington was the route's first car ferry and is seen loading at the slipway adjacent to Lymington Pier station while the Freshwater is on stand-by. (John Hendy collection)

The Lymington is seen late in her career with a Ford Anglia boarding at Lymington slipway. The car is driving onto the ship's ramp over a pair of wooden boards which were necessary in order to prevent vehicles grounding. On the left, passengers make their way into the station. The ship's passenger lounges were built in sponsons in the style of the earlier paddle steamers. (John Hendy collection)

in the following September was purchased by H.G. Pound's scrapyard at Portsmouth thereby never operating for the nationalised British Railways Board which took control of Britain's railways on New Year's Day 1948. She finished her days serving as 'Bert's Cafe' alongside the A27 at Porchester and in this role lasted until 1958. June 1951 saw the two-class system abandoned on the railway-owned Isle of Wight ferries.

By 1955 the number of cars being shipped on the passage had risen to 42,000 and it came as little surprise when the order for a third car ferry was made. The new Voith-Schneider propelled *Freshwater* came from the Ailsa yard at Troon and entered service on 21st September 1959. With capacity for 620 passengers and 26 cars, she was not quite so large as the *Farringford* but settled quickly to work the route with her companions – a state of affairs which was to exist until the close of the 1973 season. The *Freshwater* was the last Isle of Wight ferry to be fitted with deck sockets for sheep pens and until the mid-1960s livestock continued to be carried 'on the hoof' rather than in lorries.

In preparation for the arrival of the new ferry, the route's final

The year 1973 was the twilight of the route's first generation car ferries as the Yarmouth-bound Farringford (left) passes the Lymington on 20th August. (John Hendy)

The Lymington unloading at Yarmouth during her final season. (John Hendy)

The route's second Freshwater on the lay-by berth at Lymington on 14th April (Easter Day) 1968 as the Farringford creeps up to the slipway. Cars for shipment are lined up on the right in front of the level crossing gates. (John Hendy)

paddle steamer, the Freshwater of 1927, briefly became the Freshwater II before being withdrawn from service on 18th September 1959 and laid-up at Southampton. During her final seasons, she was used very sparingly, operating on Saturdays carrying passengers to and from Island holiday camps. She was later purchased for excursion work firstly at Brighton and then in the Swanage-Bournemouth areas becoming the Sussex Queen and then the Swanage Queen but was not a success and was finally sold to Belgian breakers in May 1962.

The Lymington was often used to deputise on the Portsmouth – Fishbourne route during periods of overhaul and was even used on

This view of the Lymington berthing at Yarmouth on 20th August 1973 really does serve to illustrate how small she was by today's standards. She carried just two lanes of traffic but with a single lorry using both lanes, her capacity became severely impaired. (John Hendy)

Alresford. The electrification of the London – Bournemouth line saw as much as 40 minutes lopped from the 98-mile Waterloo – Lymington service and a resultant increase in passenger numbers. At this time, over half of all passengers travelling to the Isle of Wight on British Rail routes used the Lymington – Yarmouth service. Following a short period of diesel operation, electrification of the Lymington branch line took place on 2nd June 1967.

As the 1960s drew to a close, improvements were finally put in hand to enlarge the shore facilities at both Lymington and Yarmouth as cars carried in 1967 had reached 109,000. At the same time plans were announced for two new ships. The frequency of crossings was

The route's first car ferry, the Lymington, could latterly accommodate just 16 cars. (John Hendy)

the Portsmouth - Ryde route for four crossings in March 1967. In 1964 the other two car ferries underwent trials on the Portsmouth – Fishbourne route although the *Farringford* proved unsatisfactory at Fishbourne's slipway.

In March 1965, work started at Yarmouth to extend the slipway in order to make berthing easier at low water. Other improvements were occurring ashore when on 2nd April 1967, the last steam-hauled trains were operated on the Lymington branch line. Locomotive 41312 is today preserved on the Mid-Hants Railway at

The diesel-electric paddle vessel Farringford arriving Lymington in July 1971 and illustrating the advances in her design with far larger passenger lounges. Note the raised gangway that linked the port and starboard deck areas. (John Hendy)

The diesel-electric paddle vessel Farringford *leaving Lymington in July 1971. (John Hendy collection)*

increased to cope with all the extra traffic on offer and in order for this to be achieved, in 1971 dredging in the Lymington River was completed to allow two vessels to pass each other within its confines. The work took five minutes off the crossing time and during 1972, services were stepped up to half-hourly during weekends in July and August.

In August 1973, the *Freshwater* was used to test the local afternoon cruise market when on Tuesdays and Thursdays she took passengers to the mouth of the Beaulieu River and across to Cowes. On Wednesdays she sailed to the Needles and there were even two trips to see the Cunard liner *Queen Elizabeth 2* in Southampton Water.

Further unusual work was found for the *Cenred* when she tendered to the Swedish liner *Kungsholm* off Ryde on 12th May 1974 while the *Freshwater* was used for similar purposes in January 1971 tendering to the liners *Randfontein* and *Pasteur* in Cowes Roads.

Prior to the arrival of the 'C' Class, the Portsmouth – Fishbourne ferry *Cuthred* did trials on the Western Solent link. Built at Lowestoft in 1969, her hull was similar to that of the new ships and apart from serving as an operational exercise, it also helped to allay the fears of the yachting community who were claiming that the new ships would be too large for the Lymington River.

THE 'C' CLASS

Three identical sister ships costing a total of £1.8 million, were ordered from the Robb Caledon yard in Dundee, the first for the Portsmouth station and the other two for Lymington. By this time, the ship naming policy of the British Railways Board had changed from the familiar 'local' names to those of rather obscure historical characters from the period known as the 'Dark Ages' and who appeared to have few links with either the New Forest or the Isle of Wight! Caedmon was a monk and the earliest English poet who lived at Whitby Abbey in the seventh century while Cenwulf and Cenred were Anglo-Saxon Kings of Mercia.

The 190 feet long *Caedmon* was launched on 3rd May 1973 and initially boasted accommodation for as many as 750 passengers with 52 cars on her vehicle deck. Launched by Lady Taylor of Gryfe (wife of the Chairman of B.R. Scotland) the new ship completed her maiden commercial voyage on 27th July and became the Fishbourne

Following the launch of the Cenred into the River Tay at Dundee's Robb Caledon yard on 3rd July 1973, the vessel was towed down river to the fitting-out yard. (Dundee City Archives)

route's much-needed fourth car ferry.

The *Cenwulf* was the first of the new Lymington vessels and was launched by Mrs. Cobb, the wife of Sealink's Chief Commercial Manager (Irish & Estuarial) on 1st June making her maiden voyage on 18th October. She replaced the pioneering car ferry *Lymington* which was officially withdrawn on 9th November.

The third of the new trio of ferries was the *Cenred*, which although named by Mrs. Janice Barwell (wife of Sealink's Superintendent Engineer-in-Chief) on 29th June was prevented by gales from being launched until 3rd July. On her journey down the North Sea she encountered some heavy weather and had to put into

The Cenwulf in her original Sealink livery is seen on passage to Lymington during 1979.
(John Hendy)

Great Yarmouth before proceeding south. After a two-month spell on the Portsmouth – Fishbourne route, she entered service at Lymington during late January 1974 replacing the *Farringford*, which had been withdrawn on 8th November before being sent to the Humber to operate the Hull – New Holland service. For this work she was converted to side loading operation and commenced the final phase of her career on 4th February 1974 lasting until the opening of the Humber Bridge on 24th June 1981.

The *Freshwater* meanwhile was retained as a relief and summer back-up ferry until her own withdrawal at the close of the 1983 season. After receiving side-loading gates during her refit at Southampton during autumn 1978, in January 1979 and 1980 she travelled northwards to the Humber to relieve her former Lymington fleet companion *Farringford*. The journey to the Humber in January 1980 saw her put into Dover with engine problems. The ship was also used as a winter relief on the busy Portsmouth – Ryde passenger service but her limited catering facilities and lack of speed meant that she was far from being an unqualified success and train connections were often missed. During her February and March stint in 1982, extra accommodation was supplied in the form of two old Southern Vectis coaches parked on her vehicle deck.

Curiously, the *Lymington*, *Farringford* and *Freshwater* all eventually passed into the ownership of Scottish operators Western Ferries (Argyll) Ltd. for their 20 minute crossing of the upper Firth of Clyde. The *Farringford* was never to operate for them and was scrapped at Hull during 1984. In 1988, the former *Lymington* (by then renamed *Sound of Sanda*) celebrated her fifty years in service – an amazing record for a ferry of her type. She was finally withdrawn in

The new Lymington twins Cenred and Cenwulf (astern) are seen at Robb Caledon's fitting-out yard on 17th July 1973. (John Hendy)

1989 and after an attempt had failed to preserve her at Lymington, she was sold to a fish farmer on Loch Etive (near Oban) in March 1994. The old ship was eventually reduced to a hulk at Bonawe during the following summer.

The larger 'C' Class ferries on the Lymington – Yarmouth route generated their own traffic and during their initial twelve months shipped 179,000 cars while a million passengers were carried for the first time.

The fitting of mezzanine decks during 1977–78 increased car capacity by 18 at peak periods while the construction of linkspans at

The Caedmon was the first of the three new ships in service and for her first ten years was used on the Portsmouth - Fishbourne route. She is seen running into a south-westerly gale while crossing to the Island in September 1978. (John Hendy)

Lymington in 1975 and at Yarmouth in 1983 enabled speedier turn-rounds and easier embarkation for the increasing flow of heavy vehicles using the passage.

The new £250,000 Lymington terminal involved the reclamation of land to the east of the railway pier during 1972-73. The £100,000 linkspan cost almost as much as the projected repairs to

the original slipway but allowed easier berthing and loading and also cut down on maintenance costs. The major problem with the 1938 slipway was that it was on the wrong side of the railway line which allowed an insufficient standage area for only about 20 cars waiting to embark. The remainder had to wait on the shore side of the level crossing gates and because the ships' timings coincided with those of the trains, motorists had been known to miss their sailings. In order to accommodate the new linkspan, the railway line was shortened by about 60 feet. A covered passenger walkway was also constructed alongside the linkspan through which passengers were able to walk directly into the ships' accommodation via mechanical gangways thereby eliminating the need to use the old manual gangways. The new terminal was opened in January 1976.

CELEBRATION

In June 1980, the route held a day of celebrations to commemorate the 150th anniversary of its inception. The *Cenred* was dressed overall for the 11.30 service and crossed with a cavalcade of veteran vehicles, Morris dancers, local children in Victorian dress while a Whitbread dray was pulled by shire horses. The Lymington Borough Military Band played 'Anchors Aweigh' on the top deck.

On arrival at Yarmouth the invited guests travelled by coach for a special lunch at Farringford, the former home of Alfred Lord Tennyson. Following a serious illness in 1889, he is said to have composed his famous poem 'Crossing the Bar' during a passage to Yarmouth.

The improved Yarmouth terminal and linkspan were officially opened on 20th September 1983. In an effort to attract new business, during that year a spare car ferry was used on Wednesdays for three-hour cruises between July and September and was also available for charter with a maximum for 300 passengers. Refurbishment of the three 'C' Class saw each vessel being given its own colour identity.

The entry into service at Portsmouth of the St. Catherine and St. Helen

during 1983 rendered the *Caedmon* surplus to the Fishbourne route's requirements and she was moved westwards to join her sisters during November.

The denationalisation of Sealink UK Ltd - the shipping subsidiary of the British Railways Board - took place in July 1984 when the fleet became part of the Bermuda-based Sea Containers. The ships reflected this by being marketed under the banner of Sealink British

The Freshwater *remained in service as the third ship until the* Caedmon *was released from the Portsmouth station in November 1983. Seen from the incoming* Cenwulf *in August 1979, the older ship had previously vacated the linkspan before proceeding down river to Yarmouth. (John Hendy)*

In the early evening light of 20th August 1987, the Cenred (left) heads down the Lymington River to Yarmouth as the inward bound Caedmon prepares to pass her. With Lymington Pier station in the foreground, this view illustrates the river's meandering nature and the constant hazard of yachts in the narrow waterway. The Island's western downs make a fine backdrop. (John Hendy)

Ferries. The Lymington – Yarmouth route had remained railway-owned for exactly a century.

With the *Caedmon* now in operation with her sisters in the Western Solent, the *Freshwater* was sold to Portsmouth ship breaker H.G. Pound. There she languished before purchase by Lebanese owner Anis Abiad who apparently intended to operate her on a most

unsuitable fifty-mile route linking Cyprus and the Turkish mainland. Rumours followed that the vessel was really intended for the Lebanese Christian Militia in Beirut but whatever the truth, the old *Freshwater* remained on her berth before being sold again in late 1985 to Western Ferries, becoming their *Sound of Seil* and commencing service on the Firth of Clyde on 18th June 1986. In this role she

The former Portsmouth - Fishbourne ferry Cuthred at lay up pending sale at Lymington in August 1987. The vessel's design was the precursor for the 'C' class and she carried out trials on the western Solent link. (John Hendy)

gave ten more years' service before finishing in July 1995 and being passed to a Garston (Merseyside) scrap yard in summer 1996 for conversion to a crane barge. Even more surprisingly perhaps, the scrap yard went into liquidation shortly after starting to dismantle her and the wreck survives, abandoned and with her back broken on the Mersey shore; a sad end for the vessel which for 14 years had been Lymington's top ship.

Following the takeover of the Sea Containers (Sealink British Ferries) ferry division by the Swedish Stena Line, the Isle of Wight services were excluded from the sale and remained with the Bermuda-based company. Now unable to continue using the Sealink trading name, Wightlink was created in November 1990.

Five years later, in June 1995, a management buy-in backed by the Royal Bank of Scotland and venture capital company CinVen made Wightlink totally independent and in October 2001, the company's management bought-out CinVen's interest.

More changes were occurred in 2005 when the Australian-based Macquarie European Infrastructure Fund Group acquired Wightlink.

After the route's first car ferry Lymington was sold to Western Ferries, she was renamed Sound of Sanda for service across the Firth of Clyde. (John Hendy collection)

The Freshwater of 1959 as she looks today - partially broken up at Garston on Merseyside. The breakers went into liquidation before they could complete the task of dismantling her. (Richard Seville)

A change of livery was introduced after 1984 when Sealink was de-nationalised and Sealink British Ferries was created. The Cenwulf is seen entering the Lymington River during August 1987. (John Hendy)

In 1999, the passenger accommodation of all three 'C' Class vessels was uprated and refurbished in line with work carried out to the Portsmouth-based fleet. At the time the 'C' Class was introduced (and when mezzanine decks were added in 1977-78), cars tended to be smaller and the ships comfortably carried four lanes of traffic. However, with the increase in car size this arrangement frequently became difficult and so it was decided to reduce capacity to three lanes which effectively decreased car spaces from 70 to 52. During the mid- nineties there was also a change in legislation regarding the increased provision of life rafts. As the original necessity for the large

passenger capacity of 750 had long since ceased, it was then decided to reduce this to a more comfortable 512.

In January 2003, the *Cenwulf* made her first appearance on the Portsmouth – Fishbourne route using the old slipway during a period of maintenance on the nearby linkspan during which time the 'Saints' were unable to berth there.

Changes were also afoot to the Lymington railway in May 2005 which operators South West Trains decided to promote as a 'Heritage Line'. Dedicated three-car slam-door units (1497 and 1498) were repainted in the green livery of British Railways and the early blue

A good view of the linkspan, terminal and Lymington Pier station with the Cenred laying-by at the slipway berth in April 2003. (John Hendy)

Top left: The servery on board the 'Yarmouth end' of the Cenwulf. (John Hendy)

Top middle: Lymington departure showing the old slipway, Lymington Pier station and the Wightlink terminal building. (John Hendy)

Top right: The Cenwulf's main lounge. (John Hendy)

Left: The inward bound Cenwulf edges her way through the mudflats of the Lymington River. (John Hendy)

On board the Wight Light. A view from the bridge of the Lymington River with its neatly moored lines of yachts. (John Hendy)

The Cenwulf edges past the Cenred iin the Lymington River. (John Hendy)

and grey colours of British Rail and were renamed 'Farringford' and 'Freshwater' thereby reviving the memory of the former ferries.

Meanwhile, with the three 'C' Class ships approaching an age at which retirement might be expected, they were being worked harder than ever right around the clock and were frequently found to be capacity constrained during the summer peaks.

It would be wrong to think that the careers of these three stalwarts has just involved ferry work between Lymington and Yarmouth as occasionally they have been used for cruises and special events including the *Caedmon's* cruises during the 1980s to the Cowes Fireworks, the *Cenwulf's* D-Day Fleet Review cruises in 1994 and the *Cenred's* 'one-off' cruise to the Needles at the time of Captain Andy

Lavies' retirement. Mindful of the possibility of ramp failure at Fishbourne at which time the dedicated 'Saint' Class ships would be unable to operate the route, in recent years all three of the versatile 'C' Class ferries have undertaken trials at the old slipway.

Much work had previously taken place drawing up plans for new ships but the route is difficult, the Lymington River forms part of an environmentally very sensitive area and many important issues have been considered during a long consultative and design process.

The new 'Wight' Class ships represent the culmination of many years' endeavour and are set to carry the Wightlink banner on the Western Solent long into the foreseeable future.

Name	Entered service	Disposal	Gross Tonnage	Length (metres)	Passengers/Cars
Glasgow	1830*	1849	51	16.5	No information
Solent (I)	1841	1861	61	25.8	No information
Red Lion	1858**	1879	54	23.6	100 approx
Solent (II)	1863	1901	61	26.1	230 approx
Mayflower	1866	1905	69	30.1	250 approx
Lymington (I)	1893	1929	130	37.0	311 summer/236 winter
Solent (IV)	1902	1947	161	41.1	398
Carrier	1906ß	1931	98	18.7	Tug & cargo vessel
Freshwater (I)	1927	1959	264	48.8	500
Lymington (II)	1938	1973	275	45.5	430/20
Farringford	1948	1974	489	54.8	320/32 or 800 pass.
Freshwater (II)	1959	1983	363	50.5	620/26
Cenwulf	1973	2008	746	57.9	512/52
Cenred	1974	2009	746	57.9	512/52
Caedmon	1983***	2008	746	57.9	512/52
Wight Light	2008		2,546	62.4	360/65
Wight Sky	2008		2,546	62.4	360/65
Wight Sun	2009		2,546	62.4	360/65

* The *Glasgow* was built in 1828

** The *Red Lion* was built in 1856

***The *Caedmon* entered service on the Portsmouth – Fishbourne route in 1973

ß The *Carrier* was built in 1904 and was converted to a barge in 1931

Gross Tonnage is the usual method of measuring merchant ships and refers to a ship's volume – 1 gross ton = 100 cubic feet.

Sources differ concerning the withdrawal from service and disposal dates of selected earlier vessels which in some cases were several years apart.

BUILDING THE 'WIGHT' CLASS

Much has happened since the 'C' Class ferries entered service in 1973. This not only involves changes in the nature of traffic but also in advances to technical and mechanical matters and the imposition of new and far tighter safety regulations.

The new 'Wight' Class ferries will offer a far greater flexibility than the ships they succeed. They will not only be capable of carrying a greater and more varied traffic load but the decrease in the number of passengers will reflect the inevitable move from the time-honoured train-connected foot passenger trade to those who now travel by car. Yet interestingly, the passenger areas in the new ships are both larger and offer more facilities than have been seen previously; their modern and attractive passenger lounges will be a tremendous improvement in terms of space, design and functionality.

The interior design is the work of LAP Architects of Billericay in Essex although the actual fitting-out has been completed by a specialist company in conjunction with the Croatian builders. The designers' aim was to create a light, airy and colourful interior, giving plenty of space for passengers yet at the same time ensuring comfortable and functional public areas.

The new ships will be far more fuel-efficient than the 'C' Class and will offer greater flexibility and capacity for transporting cars and commercial traffic.

New regulations involving safety at sea now require a far higher level of damage stability which was a major factor in deciding to replace the old 'C' Class. It was therefore necessary to increase the length of the design by a modest 4 metres and the width (beam) by

The launch of the Wight Sun. The third vessel in the trio is due to enter service at Easter 2009. (Wightlink)

just 80 cm. This, say Wightlink, will help to secure the long-term financial viability of the service and enable the traffic mix to be transported more efficiently. Not only will the increased proportions allow the ships to fulfill the latest requirements but will also allow them to carry 15 more cars than the ships they will replace. They will be powered by four main Volvo D16MHs 6-cylinder engines which will drive 2 Voith-Schneider 21 R5/135 propeller units.

Throughout August 2006 tenders for the building of the new ships were sought from a number of European yards and were considered during October before contracts were agreed with the

The second of the series, Wight Sky, *is seen shortly after her launch on 12th April.* (*Wightlink*)

The Wight Sun *was built on the same slipway as the* Wight Light *and is seen fitting out during July.* (*Wightlink*)

Brodogradiliste in Kraljevica during December 2006. These were not enforced until 20th March 2007 after which Wightlink was committed to build the new £10 million ferries in Croatia. The yard is owned by the Croatian Government and is one of Europe's oldest established facilities with a history of shipbuilding dating back to 1729.

With due ceremony, the keel for the Wight Light (Yard number 550) was laid according to schedule on Tuesday 26th June 2007 while the keel for the second vessel Wight Sky (Yard 551) was laid alongside in early August.

As work continued in Croatia placing some 700 tons of steel to construct each ship, in early November came the announcement that Wightlink had ordered a third new ship for the route. Due for completion in November 2008, the Wight Sun should enter service before Easter 2009 but as construction was to take place on the same slipway as the Wight Light, work was unable to start until after she was launched.

Until this time in the process of introducing the route's new tonnage, Wightlink had simply referred to the vessels as the 'R' Class - after Rona, a member of the Lymington team – but decided to hold a competition to choose the names of the three vessels. Hundreds of people participated and the winning names were revealed on 5th November. These sprung from the imagination of 51-year old former Customs Officer Mark Southwell from Cowes who chose the names, *Wight Light*, *Wight Sky* and *Wight Sun* as he wanted them to reflect something of the character of the Isle of Wight. From now on, the ships became known as the 'Wight' Class.

In order to allow a correct port fit, the berth at Yarmouth was modified from Easter until late May, when the slipway was again

activated, thereby allowing the linkspan to handle the 80 cm increase in freeboard. Lymington's linkspan later followed suite.

The first of the trio, the *Wight Light* was launched with due ceremony on Saturday 26th January by local 7-year old Nevia Pravdica who cut a chord which released the Champagne bottle and the hydraulic rams which held the ship in place on the slipway. It had previously come to light that the ship was actually 85 mm shorter and 35 mm narrower than specified. The discrepancy was put down to the fact that welding took place during a hot Croatian

An attractive glass screen, showing an antique map of the Isle of Wight, separates the ships' retail outlets from their comfortable accommodation. (John Hendy)

The lounge at the Yarmouth end of the new ferries, offers passengers magnificent views of the western Solent. (John Hendy)

Nudging up to the lay-by berth at Lymington after her morning trials on 18th September, the Wight Light is passed by the incoming Brockenhurst electric multiple unit 1497, 'Freshwater'. (John Hendy)

summer when the steel had expanded. Immediately the ferry was in the water, anchors were dropped to slow her weigh within the confines of the shipyard before a tug nudged her towards the fitting-out berth. Within hours of the launch, the keel of the *Wight Sun* was laid on the same slipway when the senior Lymington Master, Captain

Guy Digby performed the traditional good-luck ceremony by fixing a coin to the seven tonne section. The second ship, *Wight Sky* went down the ways on 12th April when seven-year old local girl Nika Radovic performed the ceremony. Extensive sea trials were carried out before the ships were accepted and although originally a late

The Wight Light is seen passing the Royal Lymington Yacht Club as she approaches Lymington Pier at the end of a trial run from Yarmouth. (John Hendy)

The Yarmouth end of the Wight Light's comfortable passenger accommodation. (John Hendy)

Out on deck and looking up at the Wight Light's full width bridge which was raised by 1.8 metres during the construction process in order to give the Master unparalleled all-round views. (John Hendy)

May arrival was anticipated, due to delays in the shipyard this was later deferred until August.

The launch of the *Wight Sun* occurred on Saturday 28th June with a local schoolgirl, Stefani Nahdoh, performing the ceremony. A visiting team from the Lymington – Yarmouth route were on hand to witness the event and later visited the *Wight Light* which was by then in the advanced stages of fitting out. The launch coincided with the publication of an independent report into the environmental impact of the replacement fleet for the Lymington-Yarmouth route. The report, by the Marine Environmental agency ABP Mer supported

Wightlink's original assessment and concluded that the new ships would have no greater adverse environmental impact than the existing fleet.

Although it had originally been hoped to sail the first two of the trio home together, as the summer of 2008 drew on it became increasingly obvious that this would not occur. The *Wight Light's* sea trials took place over two long days, each spanning a period from 08.00 until 02.30 the following day, and were supervised by Colin Stanton, Wightlink's Project Manager at Kraljevica shipyard.

The *Wight Light's* speed, determined over a measured mile in both directions, was calculated by the Zagreb Institute of Shipping to be 12.39 knots. Ship handling was tested and found to be excellent while the vessel's systems and navigation aids were also subjected to thorough examination. After dark, for example, emergency equipment and lights were tested in black out conditions.

Echoing the results of the independent environmental report commissioned by Wightlink and announced earlier in July, the sea trials confirmed that very little wash was produced by *Wight Light* at speeds of up to six knots and that what was seen compared extremely well with the 'C' Class vessels.

The first of the trio of new ferries eventually sailed for England for her sixteen day voyage on 15th August calling at Gibraltar en route. The *Wight Light* is now on schedule to enter service during Autumn 2008 and after the ship had arrived at Lymington at 22.30 on 1st September, she underwent further trials and crew operational training on the Solent. Harbour authorities at Lymington and Yarmouth then monitored her performance before procedures were finalised and a date confirmed for the *Wight Light*'s entry into service.

Looking down the Wight Light's main vehicle deck showing her mezzanine deck (left) and her large panoramic windows. (John Hendy)

The new ships' bridges are particularly impressive. Senior Master, Captain Guy Digby and Captain Steve Baker (right), carry out last minute checks prior to departure from Lymington. Captain Baker delivered the ship from Croatia. (John Hendy)

OLD AND NEW – A COMPARISON

	'Wight' Class	'C' Class
Length (metres)	62.40	57.90
Beam (metres)	16.10	15.20
Draft (metres)	2.30	2.28
Max. displacement (tonnes)	1,503	850
Deadweight capability (tonnes)	348	156
Passengers	360	510
Vehicles (CEUs)*	65	52
Freight vehicle capacity** (lane metres)	110	110

*CEU = car equivalent unit

** - Freight capacity is included within overall car capacity and is not in addition to.

Displacement refers to the actual total weight of the vessel and is calculated by multiplying the volume of water it displaces by the density of the water. (This can therefore change according to whether the ship is in sea or fresh water. Warmer water is also less dense.)

Deadweight capability is the total weight of the ship in any loaded condition (including the crew, passengers, cargo, fuel, water and stores etc) minus the actual weight of the ship.

Although at maximum displacement, the new ships will draw 2 cm more than the 'C' Class, operationally it is expected that they will operate at 15 cm less than the vessels they are replacing. Around 113 tonnes of deadweight capability is surplus to requirement.

CAR/ FREIGHT CAPACITY RELATIONSHIP

	Total CEUs	Freight CEUs	Cars	Unusable CEUs
'Wight' Class	65	28	37	
'C' Class	48-52	28	4	16-20

Resplendent in the early morning sunshine, the Wight Light *alongside the lay-by berth at Lymington. (John Hendy)*

THE 'WIGHT' CLASS AND CONCERNS OVER THEIR ENVIRONMENTAL IMPACT

Of all the major ferry routes in operation around the shores of the British Isles, the route between Lymington and Yarmouth is perhaps the most environmentally sensitive. In 1975, the New Forest was designated a National Park and although the town and ferry terminal at Lymington lie outside its boundaries, the lower Lymington River and its adjacent salt marshes come very much within the park's jurisdiction.

Ever since their introduction in 1973, the three 'C' Class ferries have given sterling service to the Lymington – Yarmouth route but 34 years is a very long period of commission and they are now approaching the end of their useful careers. The stringent regulations

The Wight Sun being taken to the fitting-out berth immediately after her launch on 28th June. (Wightlink)

that govern the safety of all passenger-carrying ships are constantly being updated and if the historic route was to continue then Wightlink had no alternative but to introduce new tonnage.

It has always been recognised that the initial stages of the lengthy project to provide new ferries would require much thought, planning and dialogue as the Lymington River and its environs are environmentally extremely sensitive. The ships would therefore need to be purpose-built in order make the minimum impact on the area.

Wightlink's CEO Andrew Willson explains:

'For the extra 15 cars capable of being transported in the new ferries, the deadweight requirement is around 30 tonnes maximum. The new ferries have also been designed to carry increased bunkers and water etc., which requires a further 30 tonnes deadweight. Only around 200 tonnes of the available 330 tonnes deadweight is

The Wight Light approaching Yarmouth. (John Hendy)

expected to be utilised when the vessel is fully laden, which actually means that it should operate at a draught of less than 2.1 metres, compared to the 2.28 metres of the existing ferries.

With the placement of the propeller units on the centre-line (as compared to offset on the existing) and with a much improved hull design of the new ferries water flow is expected to be considerably more efficient, with less resultant side thrust. In addition, the vessel

A unique view of the Wight Sky, newly arrived at Portsmouth on 1st October, from the Spinnaker Tower. (John Faulkner)

has four engines for redundancy purposes. For normal running only three engines, at most, will be required, which will also be down-rated as there is a maximum power input that the propeller units can accept.

A positive feature of the new ferries will be improved fuel efficiency and lower emissions, which will comply with EU standards. The engines installed will also be capable of being shut down whilst the vessels are in berth, with a consequential reduction in noise. A closed system of cooling for the engines and generators will ensure that there is no prospect of water contamination in the river.'

In order to trial the basic design of the new ships, naval architects Hart-Fenton carried out tank experiments on a hull model in Austria. Eager to allay local fears, Wightlink agreed with Lymington Harbour Commissioners that prior to the new ships entering service, tests will be conducted to establish the safe parameters for operating the vessels in the river. It is not expected that the ships will need to operate at slower speeds within its confines but if the trials indicate that it is necessary to do so, this will probably be only at low water.

Further environmental concerns were forthcoming with regard to the effect the new ferries would have on the large areas of salt marsh on either side of the river estuary at Lymington. Wightlink's own environmental appraisal and, indeed, many studies on the erosion of the salt marshes in the Solent concluded that this is part of the natural process that is due mainly to coastal squeeze and the loss of the inter-tidal area. Studies have specifically referred to ferry wash having 'little or no effect' on salt marsh erosion. There is, however,

Yarmouth departure: the *Wight Light* heading away from the town's modified linkspan. (John Hendy)

A fine comparison between the new 'Wight' class and the faithful 'C' class as the Cenred departs from Yarmouth and the Wight Light arrives on trials. (John Hendy)

The second of the trio, Wight Sky, arriving at Portsmouth Harbour directly from Croatia on Wednesday 1st October. (John Faulkner)

The Wight Sky fitting out in Croatia when her side passenger doors for use at Lymington and Yarmouth were being tested. (Wightlink)

obvious concern about the continuing loss of the local salt marshes and further studies have predicted that they will have disappeared totally within the next 15-20 years, without some protection measures being taken. With this eventuality in mind, the Harbour Commissioners propose to create breakwaters to protect the marshes and the estuary.

A comparison between the profiles of the 'Wight' Class ferries and the ships they replace shows a larger space devoted to passenger accommodation although they will only have two decks as opposed to three in the 'C' Class. The upper car deck (Garage Deck) has been incorporated within the passenger lounge housing which is at approximately the same level as the Passenger Lounge Deck on the older vessels. For the first time on the route, there will be a lift

between the car decks and the passenger lounge.

One of the strongest and most vocal lobby groups on the Lymington River are the local yacht clubs that have voiced their concern over sailing restrictions being imposed by increased ferry traffic. This is very much a case of history repeating itself as unfounded concerns have been expressed with successive new-builds ever since the introduction of the paddle steamer *Freshwater* in 1927. Wightlink have stressed that they would not wish to see any restrictions imposed on racing in the river and that this long-standing activity should be preserved.

The fact remains that Lymington is an Open Port under the 1847 Harbour Docks and Piers Clauses Act and any vessel that can safely navigate in the harbour has a public right of access.

Farewell to the 'C' class. An unusual picture of all three 1973-built vessels together at Lymington - the Cenwulf *(left),* Cenred *(centre) and* Caedmon *(right). (John Hendy)*

ACKNOWLEDGEMENTS

The writer wishes to acknowledge the assistance provided by the following in connection with this publication: Norman Bird, Andrew Munn, John Faulkner, Keith Adams, Tom Lee, Ian Boyle, Ian Hall, Bert Moody, Andrew Cooke, Dundee City Archives, Captain Steve Baker and Steve Marshall (St. Barbe Museum, Lymington) and Stella Hendy. Miles Cowsill is also warmly thanked for his assistance with the publication's layout, production and design.

BIBLIOGRAPHY

Early Solent Steamers – Captain F.T. O'Brien
Railway & Other Steamers – C.L.D. Duckworth & G.E. Langmuir
South Coast Pleasure Steamers – E.C.B. Thornton
British Nationalised Shipping – W.P. Clegg & J.S. Styring
The LSWR in the Twentieth Century – J.N. Faulkner & R.A. Williams
Isle of Wight Here We Come - Hugh Compton
Wightlink Isle of Wight Ferries – John Hendy
The Fishbourne Car Ferry – John Faulkner
Ships of the Solent – Rigby Wason
Lymington – The Sound of Success – Alan Brown
The Lymington Branch – P. Paye
European Ferry Scene
Sealink News
Merchant Shipping Review – January 1928
Lymington Advertiser & Times – June 1980
Press Releases